MW00951157

Brenda's Bubble

Written by Eric C. Corsten
Illustrated by Megan Toenyes

Copyright 2013
All rights reserved Eric Da Goose Books

Eric Da Goose

Books

For Rowan and Presley

My name is Brenda
and I live in a bubble.

I like **BUBBLE TEA,**

DOUBLE TREES,

and to collect RUBBLE.

The others laugh at me
as I stare at stars.

They look down at me
as if I came here from Mars.

I asked my mommy

why I could not play.

She told me

I was just

made that way.

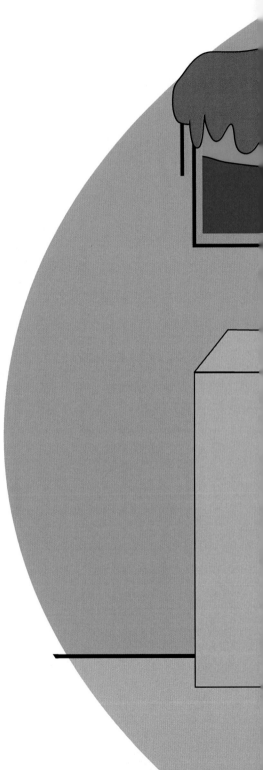

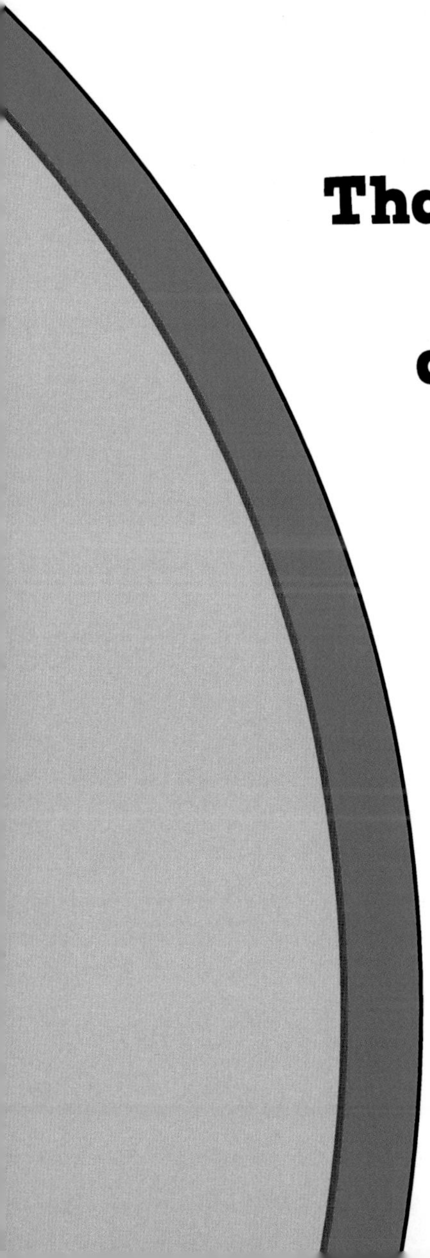

That made me feel sad

and so very alone.

I said to myself,

Bounce far from this home.

I bounced my big bubble

down to the brook.

I ate my lunch

and then a nap I took.

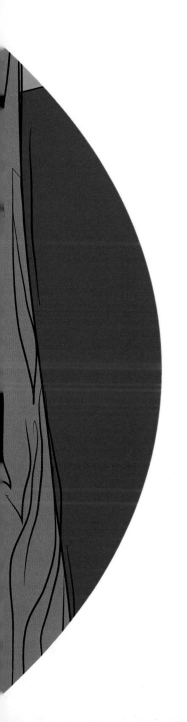

In my deep sleep

my dreams were so sweet.

Then the rain came

and I had to retreat.

It got so cold,

I sniffled and snuffled.

My bubble was there

to keep me unruffled.

I wiped the tears
that fell from my eyes.
Then a miracle happened
and it came by surprise.

I popped my bubble

while dancing around.

I had a big smile

in place of my frown.

Big bubbles are limited

Couldn't I see?

All this time trapped

When I could have been free.

Now I am free
and just like you,
I do what I want
and love what I do.

I can laugh
and sing,

or climb a tree,

hike up
a mountain,

or swim
in the sea.

There's only **one** thing
that I guarantee...

Just **burst** your bubble

and you will be **free**.

Made in the USA
Columbia, SC
31 May 2021

38528191R00015